Pianist's Pleasure
Book Two

Twenty-eight easy-to-perform
favourite melodies
arranged by Colin Hand

We hope you enjoy *Pianist's Pleasure Book 2*.
Further copies of this are available from your local music shop.

In case of difficulty, please contact the publisher direct:

The Sales Department
KEVIN MAYHEW LTD
Rattlesden
Bury St Edmunds
Suffolk IP30 0SZ

Phone 0449 737978
Fax 0449 737834

Please ask for our complete catalogue of outstanding Instrumental Music.

Front Cover: *Girl with Peonies* by Alexaj von Jawlensky (1864-1941).
Reproduced by kind permission of Heydt Museum, Wuppertal/
Bridgeman Art Library, London.

Cover designed by Juliette Clarke and Graham Johnstone
Picture Research: Jane Rayson

First published in Great Britain in 1993 by Kevin Mayhew Ltd

© Copyright 1993 Kevin Mayhew Ltd

ISBN 0 86209 478 X

Music Editor: Anthea Smith
Music Setting: Tricia Oliver

Printed and bound in Great Britain

Contents

COUNTRY GARDENS

Traditional English Melody

EINE KLEINE NACHTMUSIK

Wolfgang Amadeus Mozart (1756 - 1791)

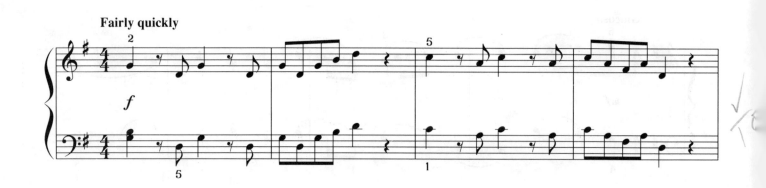

THE ENTERTAINER

Scott Joplin (1868 - 1917)

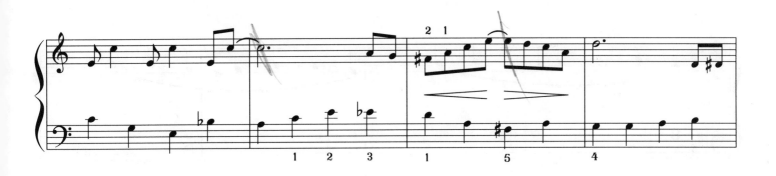

THE FLORAL DANCE

Traditional English Melody

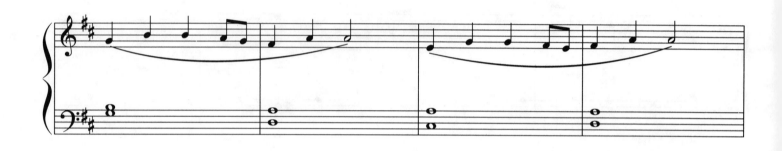

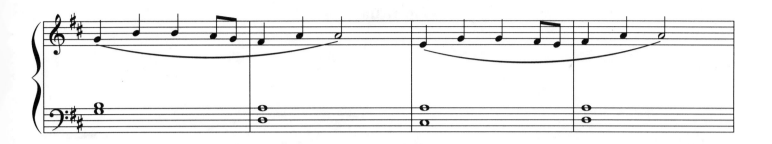

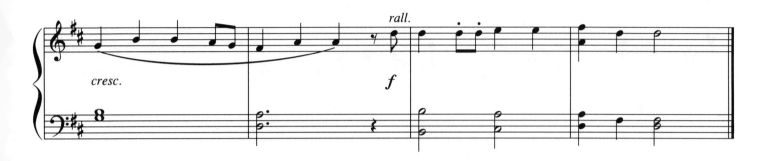

THEME from 'Abdelazer'

Henry Purcell (1659 - 1695)

DEEP RIVER

Spiritual

Fine

D.C. al Fine

GREENSLEEVES

Anon. 17th century

JEANIE WITH THE LIGHT BROWN HAIR

Stephen Foster (1826 - 1864)

PRELUDE from 'L'Arlésienne'

Georges Bizet (1858 - 1875)

THE LORELEI

Traditional German Melody

OVERTURE from
'The Merry Wives of Windsor'

Otto Nicolai (1810 - 1849)

NEW WORLD SYMPHONY (2nd movement)

Antonín Dvořák (1841 - 1904)

OVER THE SEA TO SKYE

Traditional Scottish Melody

ANDANTE from the 'Surprise' Symphony

Franz Joseph Haydn (1732 - 1809)

THEME from Symphony No. 1

Johannes Brahms (1833 - 1897)

TRUMPET TUNE

Henry Purcell (1659 - 1695)

WEDDING MARCH

Felix Mendelssohn (1809 - 1847)

RADETZKY MARCH

Johann Strauss (1804 - 1849)

GAUDEAMUS IGITUR

Traditional English Melody

ALLELUJAH

Wolfgang Amadeus Mozart (1756 - 1791)

TOREADOR'S SONG

Georges Bizet (1838 - 1875)

MARCHE MILITAIRE

Franz Schubert (1797 - 1828)

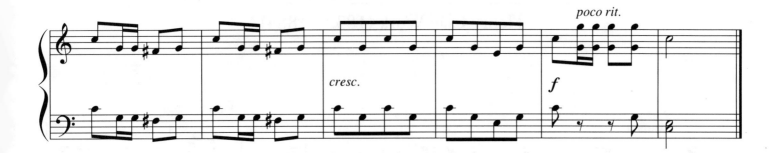

ENTR'ACTE from 'Rosamunde'

Franz Schubert (1797 - 1828)

MY GRANDFATHER'S CLOCK

Henry Clay Work (1832 - 1884)

SANTA LUCIA

Traditional Italian Melody

TOYTOWN MARCH

Leon Jessel (1871 - 1942)

SONG OF THE VOLGA BOATMEN

Traditional Russian Melody

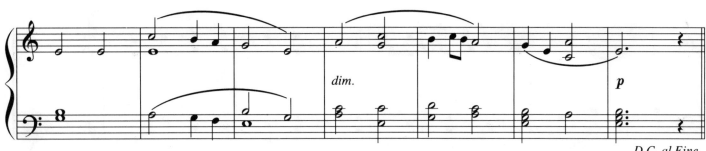

D.C. al Fine

GLORY, GLORY, HALLELUJAH

William Stäffe